C C
D1

A Selection of Words and Anecdotes
from Around Cornwall

By

Les Merton

BRADWELL
BOOKS

Published by Bradwell Books
9 Orgreave Close Sheffield S13 9NP
Email: books@bradwellbooks.co.uk
©Les Merton 2012

The right of Les Merton as author of this work has been asserted by him in accordance with the Copyright, Design and Patents Act, 1988. All rights reserved. No part of this publication may be produced, stored in a retrieval system or transmitted in any form or by any means, electronic, mechanical, photocopying, recording or otherwise without the prior permission of Bradwell Books.

British Library Cataloguing in Publication Data: a catalogue record for this book is available from the British Library.

1st Edition
ISBN: 9781902674353

Print: Gomer Press, Llandysul, Ceredigion SA44 4JL
Design by: JenksDesign@yahoo.co.uk

INTRODUCTION

Cornwall (Kernow) is the most southwesterly region of Great Britain. With over two hundred miles of coastline exposed to the sea and with the River Tamar as another boundary it makes the area where Cornish dialect is spoken more distinctly defined than any other area.

The Cornish are Celts and one of the six Celtic nations. This is probably the time to mention that the Cornish language, or Kernewek, comes from the Brythonic group of Celtic languages, which also includes Welsh and Breton. Some of the words used in Cornish dialect survived or were derived from Kernewek when the language was considered to be lost.

Today when the term Cornish dialect is used, it is understood to be a dialect of the English language spoken by a Celtic people in a Celtic territory. Sadly the days are gone when one small area in Cornwall talked in a different dialect and accent from another Cornish area. Many residents at this time could be identified by their dialect or accent as being from a certain part of Cornwall.

Today Cornish dialect speakers agree that it is a case of use it or lose it. In this book the Cornish dialect has been written phonetically in the hope that when read aloud the distinctive sound of the dialect will be heard. Sometimes the same word may be spelt differently to allow for the different accents from each area.

Les Merton

A

Aals - front room or parlour

Aar - are

Abear - Edure or dislike, I can't abear 'im

Abroad - open

Abroad - to take abroad means to take apart

Actions - pretending, lots ov actions weth shay

Addled - cracked, tha agg es addled

Adventurers - those who have shares in a mine

Aess - it is

Afreerd - afraid

Agist - against

Ain't seen 'air or 'ide obem - I've not seen him/her recently

Airy mouse - a bat

Aisy - easy

Akward like a cow 'andling a musket - a clumsy person

Alantide - All Saints' Day

Allis - always

Amenuts - almonds

Anker - a small keg or barrel used for brandy

Ansum - beautiful, good; also a term of endearment

Antic - a good - humoured fool, or a playing up action

Arrant - errand

Arter - after

A - sam - partly open

Auver - over

Av ee dun un - have you finished the job

Ax tha maid owt - ask the girl for a date

Aygar - eager

B

Babby - rags - small bits
Baal - to cry out, to howl
Back-long - before, in days gone by
Bag jis like a bucket - description of a good milking cow
Baisly - dirty, unclean
Bal - a mine
Baldag - to be spattered with slime from a mine
Beauty - can be a compliment or used as a term of contempt
Bee-butt - a bee hive
Bedwaddled - bewildered
Besting - making a decision to do something or not
Bettur a small fesh than a emptay desh - better a small fish than an empty dish (a little is better than nothing)
Bettermost - to win, to have the advantage over
Biskey - biscuit
Black fram naws ta claws - dirty all over
Blawed - out of breath, winded
Blawing House - a place where tin is melted
Blinch - to catch a glimpse of
Blunt es a dag - as blunt as a miner's axe
Booey - a louse
Bowgie - a house for sheep or a shed for cattle
Bra - great, large
Braave - first rate, hearty, good
Brae ill few - a considerable number
Bros ov het - very hot and sticky
Bucca - a ghost, a spirit or a scarecrow
Buckle to - to start to do something in earnest
Bullhorn - a snail
Bussa - a large earthenware jar or container

C

Caall 'ome - remember
Caadgin' - begging, borrowing or requesting an item
Cage ov bones - a skeleton, a very thin person
Cabby - wet, sticky, dirty or untidy
Caddle - to do housework in an untidy manner
Caan't call 'im 'om - I can't remember who he is
Cauld es a quilkin (frog) - feeling very cold
Chacking - thirsty, very dry, in need of a drink
Chamy - the profile of a toothless person
Chaunt - to scold
Cheevy - thin and miserable-looking person
Chet - a newborn kitten
Clacker - a woman's tongue
Cloam - earthenware, crockery
Clicky handed - left handed
Clucky down - lower the body into a stooping position, sitting on one's heels
Clunk et down en wan - swallow it in one attempt
Come-by-chance - an illegitimate child

C

Commis-zon - come on
Core - a shift of work
Cowal - a fish basket carried on the back and used by fish sellers
Cram - a white lie, a tall story
Creen - to grieve
Croder - a fiddler
Croust - lunch
Cudgel - a short stick, a wooden club
Cut en up a bit - able to talk posh

D

Dab - a thump or a blow
Dabbety fay! - an exclamation meaning give us faith!
Dag - a mining axe
Daggin - eager, very keen
Dear es saffern - very expensive. Sold by the dram, saffron was the most expensive item in a grocer's shop
Deep es Dolcoath - a secretive person. Dolcoath was the deepest mine in Cornwall
Desh ov tay - a cup of tea
Devilment - mischief, fun
Diddy naw en - did you know him
Didjan fer tha knockers - a morsel of food or a corner of a pasty left to appease the little people in a mine in the hope they would lead the miners to a rich lode
Dido - a fuss or a row

D

Dilly dallying - hesitating, wasting time
Dollop - a portion, a lump of anything
Dot 'n' go wan - description of a lame person
Dow - a cross old woman
Drang - a narrow place or passageway
Dreckly - a universally known dialect word, which could mean a lot longer than later

D

Dredgy ore - inferior ore or mineral
Droll-teller - a story teller
Dry - the house or room where miners change their clothes
Dull of hearing - hard of hearing, slightly deaf
Dum Dolly - a misshaped marble
Dungin' - spreading manure
Dusta - do you
Dwalling - talking in sleep or wandering in the mind

E

Eary wan week - every other week
Easement - relief
Easy - feeble minded
Eat tha sun - to bask in the sunshine
'Ed like a bladder ov lard - a bald person
Edge-on - to incite
Ee ain't gwain ta keck tha bucket yet - he's not going to die yet
Eef-ovur - half over
Ee nevur ded carrie mutch flesh bout un - he was a very thin person
Ef yew wur ta diew es yew ott ta diew - if you were to do what you ought to do
Elbow crookin' - act of tippling
Ellin stones - roof tiles
Elvan - a local variety of blue quartz, porphyry
Emmet - an ant, or used to describe tourists from outside Cornwall

E

Empty es a keg - hungry
Ent - empty, pour
Enties - empties
Es sure - agree, to be sure of something
Euchred - cornered, beaten. The term comes from the card game euchre
Evey es et - is it heavy
Evet - a newt
Eyable - pleasant to look at

F

Faace like a rusticock - red in the face
Faathur - father
Faist - feast
Fagot - a term used in Cornish wrestling for a wrestler who has agreed not to win
Fal the rals - useless things, trifles, nonsense
Fangings - earnings, wages, winnings
Feed un yew'r faace - eating
Fernaddling - stealing
Figs - raisins are known as figs in Cornwall
Figgy-duff or figgy hobbin - dough, suet and raisins mixed and baked in a pasty shape
Fitcher - ferret or polecat
Fitty - right, proper, correct
Flam new - brand new
Fleckit - squally weather
Flewers - flowers
Flies - hands on the clock

F

Flounce - to shake or jerk the body
Flummex - bewildered
Fly be nite - an irresponsible person
Foochun awaay time geekun owt ov tha winda - wasting time looking out of the window
Frange - to spread out like a fan
Freetraders - smugglers
Furrinner - someone from outside Cornwall
Full es a tick - full as a flea, eaten too much
Fulsome - food that is too rich, fat or sweet
Funkeying - a cheating move in marbles caused by moving one's arm when firing a marble
Fuzzy pig - a hedgehog

G

Gaakin - staring
Gad - a miner's pick
Gaddle - to drink quickly
Gallivanting - flirting
Gammuts - frolic, fun, play
Gashly - ghastly, horrible, unsightly
Gick nor gack - neither one thing or another
Giss on - unbelievable
Glumpy - sulky
Glutherun up - coming on to rain
Go by the ground - a short person
Gone abroad - fallen to pieces, dissolved
Gook - a bonnet worn by bal maidens at mines and clay works
Granfer - grandfather

G

Grass - above ground at a mine
Gribble - an anchor used for seine fishing
Grizzle - to grin, to show the teeth to react to something funny
Grunge - to grind the teeth together
Groushans - the dregs of tea or coffee
Gunnis - an area where a lode has been worked
Gurgoes - a long and narrow lane

Two Bal Maidens model their Gooks

Gus-up en git et fower ez wull ee - go up and get it for me will you
Gwain - going
Gwain un quietly - getting on well without making a fuss about
Gwain twentay to the dozun - rushing, doing something quickly

H

Haaf saved - half witted
Hag - a mist
Hal an tow - a type of mystery play performed through the streets on Furry Day in Helston
Hard fer 'ee izza - is it difficult for you
Hark to me - listen to me

H

Haud 'ee bal - stop talking

Haysing - poaching

Hedgyboard - a hedgehog

Hez - a swarm of bees

Hilla - a bad dream, a nightmare

Hinderment - a delay, an obstruction, a hinderance

Hisking - wheezing

Hofficer - officer

Holidays - parts or areas missed in dusting or painting

Hollow work - embroidery

Hooting cough - whooping cough

Hoppety bed - a game of hopscotch

Housing - to go gossiping from house to house

Hubba - a row, a disturbance

Huer - a look-out near the sea who shouts or signals when he spots a shoal of fish

Humdinger - something special, something very good

I

Idle - when a mine has stopped working or been abandoned

Idnt - it isn't

Iggit - idiot

Inhead - to incite

Injun stack - the high chimney of an engine house

In me nine - an eight-year-old making himself sound older

Innards - inwards, intestines

I

Inyon - an onion
Ire - iron
Ish and ish - a near thing
Iss - yes
Isself - himself
Iss fath - yes sure
Issterday - yesterday
Ivers - an exclamation

J

Jaaced - chased
Jack Harry's lights - phantom lights seen around the top of ships' masts during a storm
Jaffle - a lot of talk, a handful of hay or straw
Jailing along - walking fast
Jakes - untidyness
Jiggery pokery - up to no good
Joan the Wad - a name of one of the fairies
Johnny come fortnight - a travelling salesman
Jowds - bits, pieces
Jowlin - a gnawing pain like a bad toothache
Jump the country - to run away
Just alive - when a lode of ore can hardly be seen

K

Kail - keel
Kan Kayers - two or three confederates who unite to undervalue, tricksters
Kaping owt the road - shamefaced
Keck like a 'oss - a strong blow or kick
Keel Alley - keels is skittles, a place for playing skittles
Keenly - promising
Keenly gozzan - mining term for a promising lode
Kekezza - a type of heath
Kelter - in good condition
Kennee - can you
Kern - to curdle
Kewse - to talk
Kibbling - stealing fish
Kick up - start a rumpus or disturbance
Kicky - to stammer
Kiddleywink - a beer house, a pub
Kilt un ded - killed him
Kittle-brath - a drink made by pouring boiling water unto crusts of bread or stale bread
Knaw now do ee - do you understand now
Knuckle down will ee - give in will you

L

Labbat - a labourer that attends others ranking above him
Laity - dairy
Lambs' legs - the snivel of a child's neglected nose

L

Lasking - a fishing term which means keeping near the coast

Launder - a water shute, guttering to carry water away

Leary - faint and hungry from needing food

Leeb em diddy - did you leave him

Lemb ov the wicked - a naughty child (son or daughter of Satan)

Lerrick - to flap about

Lerrups - rags, tatters, bits

Lew - a sheltered place

Licker - large

Lick 'n' a promise - carelessly done, finished quickly, a quick wipe of the face

Like et diddy - did you enjoy that

Like Lanson Gaol - an untidy place

Lobby weather - muggy weather

Lodes - mineral veins

Longstone - standing stone or menhir

Loppin up agin - leaning against

Louster - to do labouring, to work hard

M

Mabyers - chickens

Manshun bread - small bun-shaped loaves baked without tins

Man-engine - a machine to take the miners down into a mine and bring them back up again

Mawthur - mother

M

Mazed - bewildered or even downright mad
Mazed es a brush - an eccentric person, or someone that is angry
Mazzards - black cherries
Meas - a measure for herrings; a meas is 505 herrings
Ment ut ded ee - did you mean it
Messy-y-mazy - confused, muddled
Minch - to be absent, to play truant from school
Mind em do ee - do you remember him
Miss em do ee - do you miss them
Miss the hand - to blunder, to make a mistake
Moorstone - granite
Muck owt - clean out
Murfles - freckles
Muggety pie - a pie containing sheep
Mumchance - by mere accident
Mutting - sulking

N

Nack - the right way to do something
Nag ridden - suffering from bad nightmares
Naw feer - I won't do what you ask
Naw fool behind the door - someone not easily duped
Naw un do ee - do you know him
Nawthun tearun - nothing special
Nawse - nose
Neap - turnip
New vangs - new things, something new and fanciful

N

Niceys - sweets
Night crow - someone who stops up late at night
Nimble es nine pence - a quick nimble person
Nist-un - near it
Nodder wan - another one
Nub ov sugar - a cube of sugar
Nuddick - the nape of the neck
Nuff es nuff ta mutch es a faist - enough food is all you need, too much is a feast
Nurly - sulky
Nyst - all but, nearly

O

Oarweed - seaweed
Obedullion - to chide a child
Obtain - to memorise something
Ollon a minut - hold on a minute
Oome - home
Oozle - the windpipe
Ope - opening
Oss - horse
Outwinder - a bow window
Overgone - done in, exhausted
Own - acknowledge
Owt ov core - working in one's own time

P

Padel - a dish or a pan
Padgy Paw - names for a newt or a lizard
Palchy - bad health
Pallace - a cellar for the balking of pilchards
Pard - partner, companion, friend
Pare - this usually means more than two, and it refers to a group of miners working on the pitch
Party - girl
Passel - a large number
Penny leggan - penniless
Pilth - fluff under the bed
Piskey - one of the little people, a fairy
Piskey-led - someone confused, bewildered, lost their way
Pitch to - set about doing something
Poam - to pummel, to beat
Pomster - a quack
Pop-an-towse - a fuss, an uproar
Preedy - easily, creditably
Prinked up - dress in fine clothes
Punyon end - the gable end of a house
Put en weth tha bread 'n' took owt weth tha caakes - a description of someone simple

Q

Quab - sickly
Quaff - to puff up
Quail - to wilt
Qualk - a heavy fall

Q

Quam - fainting fit
Quams - foolish ideas
Quat - to squat down
Queck sticks - soon done
Queel - to wriggle
Quiddles - foolish fancies
Quilkin - a frog
Quillaway - a stye on the eyelid
Quite es a lamb - docile

R

Rab - granite rubble
Rabblerash - a dirty and noisy mob, the great unwashed
Ram cat - a tom cat
Rames - a skeleton, bare bones
Rannish - to feel hungry
Ranny - a wren
Rantan - gadding about, going out somewhere
Raw fry - a swede, potato and bacon dish
Ream - to separate the cream from the milk
Reeming - to stretch and yawn at the same time
Reen - a steep hill
Rise in the back - to work upwards towards the mine surface
Rong es ee - is he wrong
Roper's news - old news

R

Routing-out - to clean out, to clear out drawers or cupboards
Roving pain - in great pain
Ruddy es a squirrel - as red as a squirrel, as healthy as a squirrel
Rudock - a robin redbreast
Ruff es rats - not feeling good, the morning after the night before
Rummet - dandruff
Ruxler - someone who fidgets on a seat

S

Sabby - soft and wet
Sampson - a drink of cider, brandy and a little water with sugar
Save-all - an apron that covers girls' clothes to protect them
Scabby-gullion - a stew of cut up meat and potatoes
Scads - mackerel
Scat - something that is - a slap, or something that is broken
Scrinking - looking with half-closed eyes, peeping
Scumpun - stealing
Seen un 'ave ee - have you seen him
Serv'd ee sum mane - treated him very badly
Shaip - sheep
Shigged - cheated
Shiner - a sweetheart

S

Skal - a term of abuse
Skenny - a sharp, gusty wind
Skeet - to squirt. In some areas a cup of skeet means a cup of tea
Slab - Cornish Range fire and cooking oven
Sleep - mildew
Slones - the fruit of the black hawthorn
Soas - friend, companion
Soodling - comforting, fondling, caressing
Spalls - small chips of metal or stones
Spence - cupboard under the stairs
Squeezed 'ome - shut tight
Stank - a mess. Also to walk
Steeved - broken in, forced open
Stickler - a wrestling referee
Stiddy - steady
Stramming - telling awful lies
Strub - to rob or destroy

T

Taering round - making a fuss, passionate about something
Taisy es en adder - annoyed, bad tempered
Taken lave ov yew'r senses - doing something extremely foolish
Teddy oggie - a potato pasty
Tellen bout et ded ee - did you tell him about it
Tetty-rattle - Cornish stew

T

Thase shoes es drawun my veet - these shoes are uncomfortable on my feet
Thickee 'n' thuckee - this and that
Thunder 'n' lightning - bread spread with Cornish clotted cream with treacle on top
Tidden - it's not
Timberan hill - the staircase to the bedroom
Tonguetabbis - a chatterbox
Toucher - a near hit or close miss
Towan - a dune of sand
Troil - a feast
Trowsis - trousers
Truck - trash
Tuck net - a net used for pilchards
Turn'd oogly - very cross, loss of control, in a temper
Turmut - turnip
Twadden - it was not

U

Ubben - oven
Udder - other
Ummen - stinking, very smelly
Unbeknawn - not known
Unkid - dreary, gloomy
Up long - further up in the country, or just up the road

U

Uppa uppa hoyle - follow here; term used in boys' game of foxhunting
Urge - to retch, want to be sick
Ussel - hustle
Uzzle - the windpipe

V

Vady - musty, damp
Vag ends - fag ends
Vang - a notion, a conceit, an idea
Varmut - vermin
Vean - little
Vellen - villain
Vennegar ill - looking very bad-tempered
Vestry - the smile on a sleeping child's face
Vexed - annoyed
Victor nuts - hazel nuts
Vinny - gone sour
Vlicker up - to blush
Vogget - to hop on one leg
Vore heap - a wrestling grip

W

Walkun side-waays like a crab gwain ta jail - leaning to one side whilst walking
Wance - once
Wang - to hang around in a tiresome way

W

Wan ov we - one of us, a fellow Cornish person
Want - mole
Was-sa-cum - when the speaker does not know the name of the person being talked about
Wat arre up ta en - what are you doing
Wed n - with him
Wee-wow - unsteady, confused
Whinnard - the redwing bird, or someone that is looking very cold
Whip and go - a near miss, a near chance
Whiz - a fussy person
Whimbly-wambly - feeling sick and giddy
Widdles - whims, fancying something
Wollas - lower, under
Wonders - a stinging sensation in the finger tips caused by the cold
Woss un? - what's on?
Wrasslun - wrestling
Wust aw - would you

X

Xzackly - emphasising agreement with someone say exactly (zackly)
Xzottic - exotic

Y

Yaffer - heifer
Yafful - an armful, a bundle filling the grasp
Yalla es saffern - as yellow as saffron
Yalla jounders - yellow jaundice
Yam - to eat greedily
Yap - short snappy bark of a dog
Yaw - ewe
Yet - gate
Yew - you; also a greeting
Yew doant need thet moreun a toad needs side pockets - you don't need it
Yuck - a yoke

Z

Zac 'n' zac like Tom Rawe's mouth - always correct
Zackly - exactly
Zad - sad
Zam-zoodled - half-cooked, half-baked; it can also mean the opposite, over-cooked or over-baked
Zawn - a fissure in a cliff
Zeer - worn out, aged
Zelli - a conger eel
Zighyr - when a small stream issues through a underground cranny
Zoop - to suck
Zound - faint, swoon
Zukky - to smarten up
Zur - sir

Cornish dialect words with a Kernewek (Cornish language) root

Cornish Dialect	English	Cornish Language
Bowgie	Sheep or cattle house	Bowji
Clicky	Left handed	Kledhek
Cowal	Fish basket	Kowel
Geek	Look	Gyki
Glaws	Dried cow dung used for fuel	Glos
Glutherening up	Gathering into rain	Gluthenna
Mabyer	Pullet (young fowl)	Mabyar
Planching	Plank floor	Planken
Ruddock	Robin redbreast	Rudhek
Stank	Heavy tread	Stank
Tallet	A loft	Talek
Whap	A blow	Hwaf
Zawn	A fissure in a cliff	Sawn

Numbers

The following lists give an example of numbers in Cornish language and Cornish dialect (from different areas).

Cornish Dialect	English	Cornish Language
wan, wun	one	onan
tew, toe, tow,	two	dew
dree, thray	three	try
fower, vower	four	peswar
vyve	five	pymp
sex, zix	six	hwegh
sebben, zebben	seven	seyth
aight, ate, ite	eight	eth
nyne	nine	naw
tyne, tin	ten	dek

Now that you have studied the dictionary of Cornish dialect you will be able to put your new-found knowledge to the test with this selection of anecdotes and tales that I have gathered over the years. If you are stumped over some of the words, refer back to the dictionary.

'Ow Much?

I know how important it is to be completely familiar with numbers and to have your wits about you when dealing with them. I can remember my father telling me this story of his visit to a café in Falmouth.

The waitress came over to faathur 'n' smilt, 'Can I 'elp yew?'

'Iss yew can, woss the price ov a piece ov bread 'n' buttur?' axed faathur.

'Tin pence,' the waitress replied.

''Ell!' exclaimed faathur, 'can't ford thet maid. 'Ow much es a piece ov bread weth marjareen?'

'Aight pence.'

'Naw gud,' Faathur said, after checking the money he had in his pocket. 'Tell me, my ansum, 'ow much es a piece ov bread weth owt butter?'

'Sexpence,' the waitress stated in a resigned manner.

'Thas a bit more like et,' faathur smilt. 'Tell ee what my lover, I'll ave a piece ov bread weth owt marjareen. Thet shud be onlay fower pence.'

The waitress screwed 'er faace up like a duck's fert and stanked off.

Flies on the Clock

The clock hung on the kitchen wall just inside the front door of the two-up, two-down Cornish Cottage that was my childhood home.

The flies on the clock was always kept tin minutes fast … *So we doan't mess the buzz*, Mother said. Popular visitors were told. *Doan't go yit, the clock es tin minutes fast*. Unfortunately, the less popular visitors were prompted with, *Es thet the time?* Thay left our company before they should have.

Faathur looked after the clock, winding it up at six p.m. nightly. Ee kept a small desh of paraffin enside the clock; the vapours helped ensure perfect time keeping.

Faathur liked listening to the news on the wireless. Every night when Big Ben chimed the hour, Faathur would look at the clock and say, *Big Ben es stull tin minutes slaw*.

The clock marked the time of my parents' lives, and when they passed I inherited it. The family clock was a great reminder of past happy days.

In 2005, fire destroyed virtually all of my pocessions. I found the clock buried under rubble in the shell of my former home. It was slightly fire-damaged and soaked with water from the firemen's hoses.

I let the clock dry out for about a year before I started to clean it, removing grime and dirt from its ordeal. Once this task was completed I rested the clock again, before I decided to try to get it working. I carefully wound up the clock. Nothing happened – not even a tick, let alone a tock. I started to swing the pendulum from side to side. The clock didn't want to respond…

I must have spent the next three months trying time and time again to get the clock's heart beating. One day after a push start, the pendulum seemed to get a life of its own. The clock was working. I watched the hands moving minute by minute. I decided to let the clock run until it needed winding again. When the clock stopped, I carefully rewound it. Old faithful started working, its pendulum slowly going from side to side, ticking and tocking.

The clock es pride ov place en my new home. Et es stull working. And iss, et es stull tin minutes fast…

Watch Repairers at work

Weth the Cheldren en Mind

Marbles

One marble game was known as *Towns* or *Pasties*. Before the game commenced, an important decision had to be made, whether to play for *Keeps* or *Poors*. *Keeps*, the winner kept all the marbles won in the game, but with *Poors*, the winner returned the marbles to their defeated owner.

Towns or *Pasties* was a complex game. I knew the game as *Towns*. However, my father said in his school days it was called *Pasties*. Preparations involved drawing on the ground, with chalk or with the steel plate on a hobnail boot heel, two crescents that faced in opposite directions and crossed one another to outline a pasty shape. Many locations were used to play marbles, from paths and playgrounds to areas of solid earth or sand. After the *Keeps* or *Poors* decision, tactics were shouted for: *Begs First* or *Begs Last*, depending on the marble players' preference for leading or following in the forthcoming game. Next came an even more important aspect – the rules of the game to be played. *Deads, Kills* and *Changers* or *No Deads, No Kills, No Changes,* or any combinations that got begged for:

Deads - a marble going into the town accidentally that cannot be retrieved.

Kills - allows a firing alley to be taken by another firing alley.

Changers - when in danger of being killed, the larger alley can be replaced by a small one.

The marbles to be played for were placed in the town or pasty; if only two were on offer, these were placed on the points were the two crescents crossed. If a larger number of marbles was to be played for, some of these were placed inside and some on the crescent lines.

Pinkeying Up commenced the game. Marbles were pitched from a prescribed distance, known as toeing the line, towards the town. The marble deemed nearest to the centre of the town had the right to fire first to try to knock any number of marbles out of the town. I understand the word *Drivelling* was used in certain areas to describe this opening pitch.

Sometimes a player found his marble in an impossible position for a good shot. The player could then *Beg a Move*, which meant moving in an arc around the town to get a better firing position. *Funkeying* was a method of cheating; the arm was moved forward when firing. The winner of the game was the player who knocked the most marbles out of the pasty or town.

A young boy eyeing up some new marbles in a shop window in Coverack

Mop an Heedy

Hide and seek. The Mop is the child that covers its eyes and counts while the others hide. Mopping is the term used for the child who has their eyes covered.

Ena, Mena, Out

A row of children stand facing another child, who points to each child in the row in turn and says the following rhyme:

Ena, mena, mona mite,
Bascalors, bora, bite
Hugga, bucca, bau,
Eggs, butter, cheese, bread
Stick, stock, stone dead,
OUT

The child who is pointed at when the word OUT is reached leaves the row and is out of the game, which is repeated until only one child is left.

Rhymes

Margery Daw is a well-known nursery rhyme in Cornwall, where piskies are reputed to carry off children. The nursery rhyme is recited like this:

See-saw, Margery Daw,
Sold 'er bed 'n' lay un straw;
Sha sold straw 'n' lay un hay
Piskey come 'n' carried 'er away.

Animals are popular subjects for rhymes. A bat in dialect is called an airy-mouse, and this nineteenth century rhyme is dedicated to it.

Airy-mouse airy-mouse, fly ovur my 'ead,
And yew shall 'ave a crust ov bread,
And when I brew or when I baake,
Yew shall 'ave a piece ov my wedding cake.

Food is always worth a mention; here's one description of Cornish fare:
Gurty milk and bearly-bread no lack
Pudden-skins 'n' a gud shaip's chack
A bussa o' salt pelchards, 'nother o' port,
A good strong stummick 'n' plentay o' work.

Poetry

The difference between poetry and blank verse was aptly described in Cornish dialect by this teacher of literature:

Ef yew saay:
      Ee wen up ta mill-dam
      And fell down slam.
Thas poetray.

Ef yew saay:
      Ee wen upta mill-dam
      And fell down wop.
Thas blank verse.

The Flora Dance

Helston is famous for its Flora Dance, or to be correct its Furry Dance which traditionally happens every year on or near the 8th May.

The Flora Day Dance tune is played by the town brass band and the dancers follow the band through streets that are lined with thousands of people. It is a very atmospheric day and I can remember as a child going to Helston Flora Day and seeing people crying in the streets with the emotion of it.

The noon day dance is well worth seeing; the dancers follow the words of the song and dance in and out of houses lining the streets. Furry Day celebrates the passing of winter and the arrival of spring. Helston is garland with flowers and many locals wear a lily of the valley in their button hole.

Couples pose for the camera

Couples dance through the town on Flora Day

Anecdotes

Fower ov uz wen' down Viskey ta git a pennith of bran, took geat sticks weth uz wudden a bit afreed yew.

Un faathur's berthdaay, ee raychieved a parcel fram es boy et contain'd a 'at 'n' a note whech rid; Happy Berthday Faathur, ef the 'at doan't fit, yew can cum ovur un Saturday 'n' we'll go enta tha shop en chaange et. Doan't forgit ta breng your 'ed measurements weth ee.

The passon axed the church-warden ta spread dung roun' the base of the church tower ta help the ivy grow. A passerby thought ee waas dungin' the tower ta maake et graw taller.

Sport

Cornish Wrasslun

Wan ov the geat Cornish sports was wrasslun. Thus waas played oall over Cornwall, weth evidence ov ets exsistence gwain back to the Battle of Agincourt in 1415. Every match starts with a quote in Cornish language: Gwari hweg yw gwari teg -
Fair play is good play.

'The stickler keeps a close watch as the wrestlers try for a winning hold'

A Day In The Life Of Ivor Denbal

'Woss on en, me ansum?' Ivor Denbal stopped straining and looked in the direction of the voice. It belonged to Constable John Pascoe, known locally as Long John on account of the underwear he wore unofficially under his police uniform. The very same underwear his wife advertised, as a true example of her husband's whiter-than-white police record, every Monday on her washing line outside the police house in Penfibber.

'Nawthun,' Ivor Denbal replied, standing up straight in the dustbin.

Long John took out his notebook, looked at his watch, licked his pencil, and started to recite as he wrote.

'On Friday, the first of April, at eleven a.m. whilst patrolling the lane that runs west of the post office in Penfibber, I saw a person known to me as Ivor Denbal standing in a dustbin. He was straining at the dustbin handles. When asked what he was doing, he said, 'Nawthun' in a dialect that confirmed he was a resident from the bottom end of the village.'

Police Constable Long John Pascoe licked his lips and dropped his official Police English. 'I sid, woss on? Yewr standun en thet dustbin like tha village idiot. Naw, I didun mane thet. When they sent yew ome fram St Lawrence's, yew ad a certificaate ta saay yew waas sane.'

As if that was his cue, Ivor Denbal gripped the dustbin handles and started to strain. His face went bright red with the effort. He let go of the dustbin handles and let out a long sigh.

''Tis naw gud, Long John, I mane Mistar, I mane Constable Pascoe.'

Thinking this could be a breakthrough in crime detection, Long John Pascoe licked his pencil and said,

'Come on, son, you can tell me all about it. Why don't you step out of that dustbin and come for a cup of sugary tea down at the nice, very nice, police house?'

'Caan't.'

'What do you mean, young man?' Constable Pascoe asked with true police efficiency.

'Caan't.'

'Don't caan't me!' Long John exclaimed and gave Ivor a quick clip under the ear.

'Yew caan't et me en tha chacks. I'll 'ave tha law un yew!' Ivor shouted.

'I am tha law, you saffron bun short of a tea-treat!' Police Constable Pascoe snapped. He sneered, 'I'm arresting you for being a public nuisance.'

'Caan't.'

'Can,' replied Long John, getting out his handcuffs.

'Caan't,' Ivor repeated, gripping the dustbin handles and straining upwards again. 'I'm trainun, I am, I'm trainun.'

'Trainun?' asked the bewildered policeman, 'Training? Training? What are you training for?'

Long John held up his hand for silence. This, by the way, is the same signal as the prescribed signal police use to indicate motorists to stop. He put his handcuffs away and proceeded to bring his notes up to date.

He narrated, 'I asked the person known to me as Ivor Denbal what he was training for.' Police Constable Pascoe smiled the smile he always smiled when the judge said, 'Take him down, officer.'

'Training?' the police officer cross-examined cunningly.

'Trainun. Trainun ta bay a wraslar.'

'What?'

'I'm trainun ta bay a wraslar.'

Long John paused, and the cogs of police methods of interrogation slipped into gear. He asked in procedure mode, 'All-in wrestling or Cornish wrestling?'

'Both,' Ivor replied with a smile that didn't make him look quite fitty, followed by a grunt as he strained at the dustbin handles.

'Please explain in full detail.'

'Wraslars 'ave gotta bay strong ta lift tha other bloke. Percy tha Postman sid ta bay a wraslar I 'ad ta bay strong 'nough ta lift myself up whilst I waas standun en a dustbin.'

Police Constable John Pascoe drew himself up to his full height (one hundredth of an inch below the minimum police regulation height - he stuck hairs to the soles of his feet for his police entrance examination and got in by a whisker).

'Ivor Denbal, I am arresting you on suspicion of wasting police time. I must remind you that anything you say may be taken down in writing and used as evidence against you in a court of law. Do you understand?'

Ivor Denbal's mouth went abroad like a fish out water. He nodded.

'Good.'

Long John put away his note-book and pencil and pulled out his police whistle. He made a long exaggerated attempt to blow it. Not a single note came out. John Pascoe took the police whistle out of his mouth and held it up to the light. He shook his head in dismay. Ivor watched in silence, his curiosity growing more and more by the minute.

'The reason I tried to blow my police whistle is that I need help to take you and the evidence,' he pointed to the dustbin, 'down to the police station. However, the pea seems to have fallen out of my whistle. Seeing as I can't summon any of the aforesaid help...'

Police Constable Long John Pascoe paused for dramatic effect (for a definition of dramatic effect, see Police Procedure, Chapter 2, Paragraph 3), before saying, 'I'll tell you what I'm prepared to do.'

Ivor nodded, listening intently.

'I want you to get out of the dustbin, go down to the village and ask Percy the Postman if I can borrow the spare pea he has got for his whistle and bring it back to me. If you do this I'll ask the judge to take it easy on you in court.' Ivor stepped out of the dustbin and ran like a long dog towards Percy the Postman's house.

Police Constable Long John Pascoe took his notebook out of his pocket, tore out the recently written pages, and threw them in the dustbin.

All-in a days Cornish Wrestling

Drunk Logic

'Are yew sayun yew are not drunk?'
'Iss.'
'How do yew knaw when yew are drunk?'
'When I caan't tull mawthur fram faathur…'

Magistrates Clerk: 'You are charged weth 'aving ben drunk. 'Ow do ee plead, guilty or not guilty?'

Defendant: 'I waasn't drunk tall, I waas jus entoxicated.'

Rescue

All the crew of a stricken vessel had been saved. Unfortunately one seaman was brought ashore unconscious.

The new curate, who was helping, turned to the bystanders and asked, 'Ow do yew usually proceed en the case of some wan apparently drown'd?'

'S'arch es pockets,' waas the wick'd reply.

Mining

The engine houses that proudly stand against the Cornish skyline are a constant reminder that Cornwall is famous for its mines and miners, and of course for the Cornish men who travelled the world and settled many miles from home because of their mining knowledge and skills.

Here are a few mining anecdotes:

Admiration

In a sudden burst of admiration a sexton said to a mine captain, 'I'd es soon dig a graave fur yew then any man I does knaw.'

Watching

The mine captain approached an idling miner and said, 'Et do taak me haaf me time watchun yew.'

'Es thet rite,' replied the miner. 'Thas nawthen, Cap'n. Et do take me oall ov me time watchun yew.'

Pasty

A newlywed miner went home and complained to his wife, 'The pasty yew baked fer me croust, fell down the shaft and waas scat to lerrups wen et hit the ground. Wen mathur made me pasties they nevur ded thet.'

Knockers (little people)

Naw miner shud evur make a cross en a mine, cos et wull offend the knockers 'n' bring bad luck.

To appease the knockers, alwaays lave a didjen et croust time. En thenks, the knockers cud lead yew to a rich lode.

Naw whistlen es allow'd underground cos et might upset the knockers.

Not so good

Ef a miner washes es own back, ee suffer fram weakness en the back aftur.

Bad luck wull follaw a miner who turns back and re-enters es 'ome after leavun fer work.

Ef a miner meets a woman un the waay ta the pit en the middle ov the night, bad luck es sure ta follaw.

Religion

Billy Bray 1794–1868

Billy Bray was a nineteenth century miner and evangelical preacher who was known as the King's Son. His witty sayings and eccentric ways, especially his shouting, singing, leaping and dancing, caused him to become famous.

Billy Bray 'The Kings Son'. A popular Cornish Miner and local preacher from Truro. Born in June 1794 died in May 1868

When he was talking about himself in Falmouth, Billy Bray said: 'I can't help praising the Lord. As I go along the street I lift up one foot and it would say

'Glory' and I lift up the other foot it would say 'Amen'; and they keep on like that all the time I am walking.' During his lifetime he built three chapels in Cornwall.

Drinking and Tobacco

Now I tell 'ee, dearly belov'd, 'tedn' naw use ta try 'n' cure a drunkard by moderation: yew might es well tie up a touser in the gap to keep the old sow owt ov the tatties. And I don't b'lieve our Faathur meant for men to smauk. Ef a ded, a'd have put a hole en the top ov their heads: for 'tedn' no heavenly architect that'd lave the smauk go out the front door. Nor I don't b'lieve our Faathur designed women for tekkin' snuff. Ef ee did, a'd have set their noses upsy-down, for our Father meant for what we do use ov to go down 'n' not up.

In God's House

Yew won't go hungry when yew get to heaven, fer en God's house theer are many manshuns.

And a Prayer to End.

Prayer fer the Mathur-en-law
'May the Lord en es mercy
Taake ole Missues Percy
And sate 'er weth 'im un the throne
Lavun me and my Sally
En thus little valley
a live and die happy alone.'

Owt 'n' About

Thray Pints

The Pascoe bruthers, Billy, Barney 'n' Bobby, 'ad a nitely ritual; thay oal-uz arrived en the Kiddlywink et precisely tin o'clock. Thay wud go ta the bar 'n' wan ov the Pascoe bruthers wud order 'n' pay fer thray pints. The landlord wud put thray pints en front ov them. The bruthers wud go to sit down et the saame table every nite; maake a toast ov gud health 'n' drink theer wan pint ov beer each 'n' lave.

Make that thray pints plaise

Wan nite, Billy came en on es own 'n' order'd thray pints. The landlord put the usual thray pints en front of Billy, thinkun es toe brothers 'ad been delayed 'n' wud be en dreckly. Billy remain'd un es own, 'n' the landlord watch Billy down the thray pints 'n' go owt the door.

Nixt nite Billy came en agin on es own. 'Thray pints ov beer, ef yew plaise.'

The landlord put the customery thray pints en front of Billy 'n' axed, 'Un yer own Billy?'

Billy luked behind 'im, scratch es 'ed 'n' rayplied, 'Iss, thas rite.'

'Bruthers OK?'

'Iss.'

The landlord sigh'd and press'd, 'Weer be um too?'

'Worken up the line,' Billy informed.

'I see,' sid the mystified landlord, 'but yew're stull order-un 'n' drenken thray pints 'n' drenken em oall by yerself?'

'Iss, thas rite.'

The landlord hesitat'd, but 'ad ta ax, 'Why, I doan't understan'?'

Billy look'd et the landlord like ee wudden fitty 'n' eventually sid, 'I does buy a pint each fer me bruthers, saw we caan toast each othur lik weem oal-uz do.'

'Aw,' the landlord nodded 'n' went ta serve nother customer, leavun Billy ta drink es thray pints en peace.

This state of affairs carried on for a month or more, wen wan nite Billy came en 'n' sid, 'Toe pints ov beer, ef yew plaise.'

'Unlay toe pints, Billy?'

'Iss, thas rite.'

The landlord waas unable to resist. 'Barney 'n' Bobby oall rite, are um?'

'Iss,' sid Billy, picken up the toe pints 'n' wen ta sit down 'n' enjoy the beer.

The nixt nite Billy came en agin 'n' order'd toe pints.

The landlord had to ax, 'Ow cum yew use ta order thray pints, saw yer could drenk 'n' toast like yew use ta fower Barney 'n' Bobby wen ta work away, 'n' now yewr only orderun toe pints?'

Billy look'd around. Naw-wan waas wethen 'earun distance. Keepen es voice low he sid, 'Doan't tell anybody, I've ben listenun ta Billy Bray, en deci'd to geeve up drunken beer meself, but I stull want me bruthurs ta toast me like we oall-ez use ta do.'

Billy rais'd a glass, nodded, en drank et down en wan.

The Speaker's Introduction

I walked onto the small stage in the Woman's Institute, gave my winning smile when the chair lady introduced me, I started my talk.

'Gud evenun ladees. I'm luckee ta be 'ere thus evenun! Wen Mawthur knaw'd I waas cumming up 'ere to geeve a talk ta the WI, sha sid, my dear boy, 'ave yew taken lave ov yew'r senses? Yew doan't want ta go up theer ta geve a talk. Them wamen up theer wull take advantage ov a young boy like yew.'

'Wat do ee mane, Mawthur?' I axed.

'Wull yew knaw, these daays waman ov a certun age are a bit racy,' Mawthur warned and continued, 'En my daay thengs waas different. Wen yer Faathur stat'd courting me, we wen owt zix months fur we even 'eld 'ands.'

'Es thet so?' I sid.

'Iss, tiz so,' Mawthur continued, 'en then we went owt nother zix months fer I let 'im kesse me.'

'Yew doan't saay.'

'Iss, I do saay, en then we wait'd a year fer we got engaged.'

'Really?'

'Really … and do yew knaw wat happen'ed fer we cud git married?'

'I've naw idea wat happen before yew cud git married, Mawthur,' I queried respectfully.

'Wull,' Mawthur rayplied, 'yew cum along en spoil'd thengs.'

Am-bis-shun

I reckun my Uncle Fed es the onlay man ever to cheive oall ov es ambishuns. Wen es waas et school, the 'ead master axed Fed ta cum enta es office fer a chat.

'Fed, comes-es en sit down,' the 'ead master welcomed.

'Thenk ee sur,' Fed remark'd, sittun en the offered chair.

'Now Fed, thus es a very emportant question,' the 'ead master sid.

'I understand,' sid Fed en es posh voice. Fed cud cutten up

a bit wen ee 'ad to. Et waas wull knawn Fed want'd a pair ov kid gloves fer Chrissmas, so ee cud look smart; ee want'd one glove to wear and wan to flick, just like the gentray ded.

'Now Fed,' the 'ead master continued, 'I need to knaw wat am-bis-shuns yew've got fer wen you lave school.'

Now Fed waas a 'onest boy and tolt the 'ead master zackly wat es am-bis-shuns waas. Geeve the 'ead master es due ee wrote down wat Fed sid word fer word en the book supplied fer the purposs by the Ed-u-ca-shun Day-part-ment.

Years later, down the kiddley wan nite, Fed was 'aving a pint en a fag. Ee waas cussing nuff to turn the air blue bout the extra tax put un beer and fags wen who shud walk en the kiddley but Fed's old 'ead master. Ee stood behind Fed 'n' listened ta un before sayun, 'Fed, I thenk yew are my onlay pupil ever too achieve oall ov the am-bis-shuns I axed en fer en school. I remember yew am-bi-shuns waas ta drenk, smalk 'n' swear. Jus standing ere I can see yew've cheive'd oall of em. Let me buy yew a pint, yew're a credit ta the school.'

Moore un Uncle Fed

Uncle Fed waas a go by the ground – ee waas onlay fower fut nuthun. Fed 'ad summit bout un; et waas sid ee waas a ledgend en es own liftime. Ee cud thraw a sharp zex inch nale en the treble twenty aftur drunken a gallon ov sloops. Back long twas oall the raage fer Fed ta eat flewers grawun longside the road fer es croust. Wan daay ee even

49

swallow'd a worm fer devilment; aftur, ee sid the worm cum owt a 'ell ov a lot biggur.

Wan ov Fed's 'obbies waas kaping fitchers. Ee use ta take wan ov em en the kiddleywink. Sum times ef theer waas emmets en, ee 'ave a bet weth 'em ta see ef they wud put the fitcher up wan leg ov theer trowsis 'n' let et cum owt the othur wan. Take thus any waay yew like, but wen Fed brought a fitcher ento the kiddley, we wud never put es 'and en es pawkett!

Fed waas very suspicious bout the govement, en use ta get taisy bout paying tax. Ee reckun tha govement used ta put powder en custom maade fags ta make up burn faster, thas why Fed alwaays smawk'd rollies.

Ee like ta work fer cash en 'and payment. Fed wud saay cash en 'and es worth moore than the top line naw matter ow much es written on un.

Fed dedent trust banks toll, ee used taw kape any spare cash 'idden en a ole treacle tin buried owt en the garden. Ee sid ee used ta spread a bit ov dung un the garden fower times a year to 'elp es money graw.

Ee use ta go bout un a ole dunkey. Wan daay Fed went 'Elshun un tha dunkey. Gwain up Coinagehall Street, the dunkey drop down dead. Seeing wat 'appened a policeman cum up to Fed 'n' sid, 'Yew cann't lave the dunkey theer, yew'll have ta get some 'elp to take the dead dunkey down ta Church Street.'

'Why's that Hofficer?' axed Fed.

'I've gotta write a report,' sid the Policeman, ''n' I can't spell Coinagehall Street.'

Cats

'Mawthur forced the cat 'n' et died.'
'Wat ded sha force un weth?'
'Naw mait.'

Tiz sid, 'Thet a man who es cruel ta cats wull 'ave a terrible wethur et es funeral or 'ee'll be buried en a storm.'

Shrill singun es knawn es the tune the cat died with.

'Bit be bit,' the cat sid, when sha swallow'd the hatchet, 'I'll manage et, but twill be a tight fit.'

When the cat starts sneezun tiz a sign ov rain.

Mawthur's cat waas lagg'd en fleas, but sha left et be, cos et waass a gud mouser.

En the month ov May, beware – cats can bring adders unto the 'ouse.

To see a black cat un the waay ta church is consider'd to be a sign ov gud fortune. Also, ef a cat rubs against the legs ov a bride thus es consider'd fortunate.

A tom cat's tail rubb'd un an eye, es suppose ta cure a stye.

Food

Scads 'n' tates, scads 'n' tates
Scads 'n' tates 'n' conger
And those thet can't ate scads 'n' tates

O thay must die ov hunger.

Mawthur, wat ee got fer denner?
Stew'd tates 'n' barley cover
Pigeon pie es tough es leather
I waon't habben, gevun ta faathur!

Ere's a few Cornish foods to tempt you:

Muggety pie: intestines ov a pig, cut up 'n' cover'd weth onions, et's baked fer about a hour en a greased desh.

Jammy maw: es jam spread un a slice of bread.

Star gazzy pie: a fesh desh. The pie es slits en the top, so the 'eads ov the fesh can poke through and looked

A typical Cornish Range Oven with all mod cons on display

skywards. Pilchards, mackerel or herrings can be used.

Seedy cake: es a cake weth caraway seeds.

Saffern cake: a fruit cake coloured by the saffern dye. Large flat round saffern buns are also maade 'n' given owt to childern et tay treats usually organised by chapels or Sunday schools.

En talkun bout cheldern, theer waas always the mouse pasty, whech waas suppose ta be the cure for children who wet the bed.

Jaw Raw, catch'd a craw,
Put un en a pasty.
Wen ta school, play'd the fool,
And sid, 'Tiz very nasty.'

Faisten Denner

Each guest 'ad a cloam basin en front ov 'em. The guest wud crumble a slice ov nutty kettle loaf ento the basin. Faisten Brath (the liquid ov the mait 'n' veg course) waas poured ovur the nutty kettle loaf. Ate up – tiz ansum!

A dialect verse to advertise the Cornish pasty goes like this:
Wan 'n' oall, et 'unger's call
Pasties fram Cornwall
Refresh geat 'n' small
Fer denner or tay, wenever et be
Thus Cornish fare welcum'd
By wan 'n' oall.

Wan meal that kept many families gwain waas kiddley broth. Et waas sum fillun 'n' wud stick ta yer ribs ta kape the cold owt en the winter. Et waas maade by entun boilin' water unta bread thet waas well season'd weth salt 'n' pepper 'n' topp'd weth a lump ov butter. Maakes yer mouth water jis thinkun bout et. Poke up the fier 'n' pull the kittle forth.

Rechard

Et sexteen Rechard waas en tha fashun. Ee 'ad a 'air style thet waas oall tha raage: a geat quiff weth a duck's ass et tha back, 'eld en plaace 'n' shinun weth 'aircreem.

Rechard used a jar ov tha stuff everay daay. Ee dedn't wash es 'air, ee jus' 'ad a oil change,'n' ee 'ad nothur distinguishing feature – ee never 'ad any teeth, thay 'ad oall ben scat owt wan ee fell owt ov a tray wen ee waas scrumpun apples.

Gummy, greasy Rechard, ee waas a bra ole character. I lost track ov un fer years, wen I saaw en tha other daay. Ee looked sum different yew. Ee's waas es bald es a coot.

I sid, Rechard, tha shaven 'ed es uz neat uz a new pin. Ee waas like a dog weth toe tails 'n' geve me a great licker ov a smile, courtesy ov es National Health false teeth.

The Cuckoo Man

En the early part ov the twentieth century, there waas a street entertainur (ole time busker) and great local character, named George Holmes, who use to sing en 'Elson ta try ta earn a bit ov money. Unfortunately George could-nee seng ta saave es soul and consequently usually only manag'd ta collect aroun' fower pence a daay according to rayports fram the times. George waas knawn es the Cuckoo Man, es ee us ta end es performance weth the sound ov the cuckoo. 'Cuckoo, Cuckoo!'

En un the subjek ov cuckoos, when yew 'ear the cuckoo fer the furst time en spring 'n' the cuckoo calls twelve times en succession, yew'll not go short ov bread fer the rest ov the year.

"Cuckoo Cuckoo"

George Holmes - the Cuckoo man

Et es consider'd ta be lucky ta 'ear the cuckoo fer the furst time en the right ear. However, ta 'ear et fer the furst time weth the left ear … then look owt!

Muryan

The ant es alwaays ben call'd the Muryan by countray people en Cornwall. Folk-lore states thet Muryans are the small people of this earth in their state ov decay. Et es deemed ta be very unlucky ta destroy a colony of Muryans.

However, theer res wan belief thet es worth a try. Ef yew plaace a piece ov tin enta a bank of Muryan et exactly the rite moment wen the moon es full, the tin wull be turn'd en ta silver.

The Last Wolf

Once wolves existed in every part of Britain. The last wolf native to Britain lived in the forest at Ludgvan, a village just a few miles outside of Penzance. Thus last wolf waas a geat likkur ee waas a giant specimen, probablay the largest wolf ever ta 'ave exist'd. The flocks ov sheep 'n' cattle ee destroyed un a regular bases, ta fuel es appitite, had a deverstating effect un the farmers en the district. Worse waas stull ta come; the wolf waas onlay playun havoc, et waas gainun moore and moore confidence and start'd ta enter the village itself. Wan daay the wolf carried ovv a chield who waas playen en the garden ov ets parents' house.

Oall ov the community ded knaw they 'ad ta do sumtheng. They form'd a large 'unten party 'n' start'd ta track the beast, finally cornerun the wolf et Rospeith Farm un the owt skirts of Ludgvan. The wolf waas kilt dead. Life et last rayturns ta normal fer the local residents.

A Taale ov Teeth

An oald woman wen fer a walk cross the sands et Perranzabuloe en the area ov the church. During 'er walk shay came cross the remains ov sum wan buried en the sands. Shay left the bones wheer they lay but gather'd up oall the gud teeth shay cud find 'n' put them en 'er pawket.

Later thet night, wen shay wen up timberan 'ill ta bed, shay place er new found teeth collection un the dressing table. The ole womman wen ovv ta sleep. Shay waas awaken during the night by noise 'n' 'eard somewan callun owt.

'Weers me teeth? Geve uz me teeth back missus.'
Cum un missus, geve uz me teeth back.'

The oald womman tried ta go back ta sleep, but the caller waas very insistent 'n' seemed ta be getting louder.

'Geve uz me teeth back.'

'I knaw yew caan 'ear me, geve uz me teeth back!'

Tha oald woman began ta feel afeerd. Shay got owt ov bed, gather up the teeth fram the dressing table, open'd the bedroom window and thraw'd the teeth owt ento the rawd.

Naw sooner than tha teeth 'ad disappear'd ento the darkness, then 'asty retreating footsteps gwain enta the distance were heard 'n' a voice shout'd back, 'Thenks missus, I've got me teeth. Now go back ta sleep.'

The Knockers

The knockers are a part of mining history. They are considered to be the sprites of the mines. Some do say they are the souls of old tinners who are not allowed to rest and who now are paying the price for their wicked ways. These little people also worked the lodes. If treated right and given food or drink they would often lead miners to a rich lode, which in turn would enhance the miners' fangings (take-home money). By the same degree, if a miner was to upset the knockers, they would surely make the miner pay for it.

Tom Trevarrow and the Knockers

Tom Trevarrow wen ta work en a mine that waas reput'd ta be full ov knockers. Tom dedn't bayleve en knockers and scoff'd et any-wan who mention'd the little people.

Wan daay, Tom waas worken en the mine. Ee heard the sound ov others worken, but ee didn't taake any notice. Et the end ov the core, ee mentioned et to another miner went ee got ta grass. Tom waas tolt the sounds of working came fram the knockers worken a lode nearby. Tom shook es 'ed en disbayleef.

Nixt daay, Tom wen down ento the depths agin 'n' start'd work. Wethen a short time, sounds ov some-wan worken awaay en a distant part ov the mine reach'd es ears. The sounds became louder 'n' closer. Tom start'd to git a bit taisy, an ee shout'd, 'Kape the noise down!'

The sounds got louder 'n' closer. Tom waas so annoy'd, ee pick up a 'andful ov stones 'n' thraw'd 'em en the direction ov the sound.

'Git owt ov ere,' Tom shout'd. 'Ef yew doan't I'll cum over theer and scat yew'r brains owt!'

A shower of large stones waas the answer fram the knockers, wan ov wech hit Tom un the nuddick makun obem feel dizzy. Tom need'd a sit down. Ee decided ta take an early croust 'n' ta ave a touch pipe til ee felt bettur.

Tom start'd ta eat es pasty when ee heard a chorus ov voices singun.

'Tom Trevarrow! Tom Trevarrow!
Lave sum ov yew'r pasty fer uz,
Or bad luck wull cum ta ee tomorraw.'

Tom closed es ears ta the plee 'n' finish'd es pasty – even pecked up the crumbs 'n' ate em. Ee waas enjoyun a smawk until the singun start'd agin.

'Tom Trevarrow! Tom Trevarrow!
We'll send ee bad luck tomorrow,

Yew ole nasty ta eat oall yew'r pasty
'n' not ta lave a didjen fer uz.'

Tom waas afeard. Ee look'd roun 'n' saw miserable, frightnun looking little people lookun et 'im. The little people shook theer fists at 'im before disappearun es ef by magic. Tom cudden wait fer es core ta finish.

The nixt daay, Tom waas nearly killed by fallen timbers. Ee maade up es mind ta get es ard work'd fer ore up ta grass 'n' finish'd et the mine. Ee load'd the ore enta the kibble 'n' signall'd fer et to be taken up ta the surface.

Un the way up, the cable pullen the kibble snapp'd and the rich ore Tom had work'd for fell into the blackness ov the mine shaft, never to been seen again.

The curse ov the knockers had work'd. Tom left the mine weth nothun aftur oall the daays ov 'ard work.

Barker's Knee

Mister Barker waas a giant ov a man, ee wud do anytheng ta avoid a 'onest daay's labour. Nawbody knaws 'ow ee managed ta git a job down the mine, let alone kape et. Mister Barker wud go down weth the rest ov the men un es core; they miners wud oall go bout theer duties 'n' Barker wud fine a quiet spot an go ta slape fer the length ov the core. Ee waas so quiet, the knockers didn't knaw ee waas theer. The knockers wud work theer core 'n' wen it waas over, wud 'id theer tools awaay. Barker observed this 'n' thought ee wud play a joke un the knockers 'n' 'ide theer tools en a different plaace.

Nixt core, the knockers arriv'd ta find theer tools missun. Barker foun' et hilarious. The knockers eventually found theer tools and try to make up fer lost time by worken 'arder. When they finished again they 'id theer tools. Barker waas watchen, 'n' es soon es ee thought the knockers 'ad gone, ee pick'd up theer tools to 'ide em sumwheer else. But the knockers had not gone, 'n' when they saw Barker moving theer tools wan ov them grabbed a spare pick 'n' stabbed Barker in the knee with it. Barker waas in agony and screamed with pain. Thus waas greet'd weth laughter by the knockers. Until the day ov es death, Barker waas en excessive pain weth the knee; the pain waas such that et kept 'im awake around the clock.

Passun By

Walkun down the street, Ole Missus Kemp seeing somewan cumming towards 'er sid, 'I thot et were sha, 'n' sha thot et were me. Wen we cum close 'n' went ta pass wan a nuther, twudden either ov uz.'

Kind-hearted

Aunt Vi waas consider'd ta be a kind-hearted soul. Ef yew waas gwain ta kill a flea who was bitten ee, Aunt Vi wud say, 'Lebben alone, poor theng ee's onlay earnun ee's livan.'

Cut Yewr Nails

Un Mondaay fer news,
Un Tuesdaay fer a new pair ov shoes,
Un Wednesdaay fer a lettur,
Un Thusdaay fer sum theng bettur,
Un Fridaay fer sorraw,
Un Saturdaay ta see yewr true love tomorraw,
Un Sundaay 'n' the devil wull be weth ee oall week.

The Beast of Bodmin Moor

There have been many stories over the years about the Beast of Bodmin Moor. Here is a story inspired by recent sightings of the Beast.

Here Kitty

Amy Treloar waas en the twilight ov 'er years. Sha lived un 'er own en what waas wance a sheppard's cottage un Bodmin Moor. Amy spent every af-noon, weathur permitting, sitting en 'er rockun chair un the veranda ov 'er ramshackle 'ome. Amy wasn't aware thet sha 'ad senior moments ov forgetfulness, althaw occasionally 'er childhood memories seem'd so real, they took 'er to a nother age 'n' werld, that maade 'er forget 'er isolation 'n' ageing problems.

The afternoon waas like many others - warm'd 'n' relaxed by a braa many dashes ov what sha called doctor's orders brandy en 'er coffee, shay waas enjoying an af-noon nap en 'er favourite rockun chair.

A load noise thet sound'd like an enjured sheep woke 'er up weth a start. Fer a moment sha dedn't knaw wheer shay waas... the sun waas low en a sky thet waas glutherun up. The wind waas gathering strength, 'n' wethin seconds et waas a 'owling gale.

Amy tried ta focus un 'er recent dream ta bring 'er back ta reality, as sha sat theer rockun gently. Amy dedn't hear the gale or feel cold fram the temperature change. Amy waas back en 'er childhood watching sheep grazun un the open ground en front ov the cottage.

The wind died down es quickly es et 'ad start'd. The

sudden silence startl'd Amy, 'n' sha shiver'd. Sumwan's walkun un my grave, shay thought, 'n' shudder'd.

'I must be buried un a public footpath,' sha said loudly to herself as the thought ov 'er being buried un a public footpath crossed 'er mind.

Amy rocked back 'n' forth en the chair. The air waas very stull - somethun waas missin'. Sha stopped rocking 'n' look aroun'. Amy 'eard a soft chewing sound cum fram behind a bush en the garden. The bush moved 'n' what looked ta Amy like a geat likker ov a kitten emerged.

''Ere Kitty, 'ere Kitty...' Amy coaxed.

The dark, almost total black animal glanced towards the sound, before rolling un ets back en the dust. Amy waas off the veranda en a split second; she waas surprised at the weight ov the playful creature, but manages ta lift et un ta the veranda 'n' sat down en the rocking chair weth wat shay assumed waas a cat en 'er lap.

'Gud Kitty, gud Kitty...' Amy stroked the soft fur un the back ov the content'd reclining feline. Stretched owt across Amy's legs, et began ta purr softlay weth contentment. The comfort ov ets situation urged et ta stretch ets forepaws along Amy's upper leg ta the bare flesh above 'er knee. Gracefully et open et's claws 'n' stretch'd them upwards before retractun 'n' embeddun 'em en the soft bare flesh ov Amy's leg.

 Amy reacted instantly; the hand thet 'ad been softlay stroking now viciously slap the furried back en anger.

The creature spun aroun ta faace ets adversary, 'n' weth a formidable roar et leapt. The powerful fore quarters ov the beast knocked Amy back en the rocking chair weth such a force the chair toppled over 'n' the puma's owt stretch'd claws scrapped Amy's faace before the large front feet clutched the frail old lady aroun' the neck 'n' dug ets claws ento Amy's back. Holdun on weth a hunter's instinct, the puma's sharp teeth bit savagely ento Amy's wrinkled face.

Amy's terrible, high pitch, scream waas lost en the sounds ov the storm that gathered momentum; the heavy rain soaked the veranda 'n' 'elped ta wash awaay the blood.

Fish Anecdotes

Mullion Fishermen at work

The fishing industry has always been a very important part of the Cornish economy. Within the world of fishing and fishermen, Cornish dialect and Cornish language words seemed to be naturally preserved. Maybe the isolation of some of the fishing communities played its part in this. There were four main types of fishing: seining, drifting, long lining and crabbing.

Many fish have dialect names. These include: anglemaine - monkfish, capel-longer - razor shellfish, chad - a young bream, dogga - dogfish, long nose - sea pike.

Backlong wen the fishing trade waas et ets best, wan fishun village waas plagued by en abundance ov hake along the coast. Theer waas so many haake they drove awaay the profitable shoals ov pilcherds.

Wan ov the haake waas caught 'n' whipp'd before beun thrawn back en the sea. Wull thet haake musta tole the rest ov the haake bout es whippun, cos the hake vanish'd fram the area 'n' the pilcherds return'd.

Fishermen should never whistle on board a boat. Cap'n says, 'Doan't do et, cos yew'r whislun fer a gale ov wind.'

Pilchards

Twas consider'd very unlucky ta eat a pilchard 'ead furst, es thus wud drive awaay the shoals ov pilchards ovv shore. Et es essential ta start eaten the pilcherd tail furst – thus wud then encourage the shoals ov pilchards to cum close ta shore.

Many pilchards were export'd during the eighteenth and nineteenth centuries. They were salted down in the fishing areas and supplied by the thousand to Roman Catholic countries around the Mediterranean Sea, and some even went to the West Indies. This resulted in a toast from the fishermen:

Pilchard seller displaying her wares

'Ee's 'ealth ta the Pope, may ee live ta repent
'n' add 'alf a year ta the time ov Lent,
Ta teach oall ov es cheldren fram Rome ta the Poles
Theers nuthun like pilchards fer savun theer sawls.'
On economic grounds a great many pilchards went to the
Royal Navy, who called them Mevagissy ducks.

Pilcherd Palace

Geat pilcherd cellars were built near to the fishing
community harbour. Thus waas where fesh were salted fer
export. Also, for winter use fer Cornish families, pilcherds
were also press'd in the palaces fer theer oil content. Thus
oil waas knawn es train oil, 'n' wan use ov et waas fer chills
(which were earthenware oil lamps with wick made from
a rush with its skin peeled off.)

Smawk fram burnun fesh es suppose ta be a protection
against evil spirits.

Local fishermen help hold up a fence rail

Fishermen wud nevur go ta sea ef the parson or a Sally Army officer caame unta the quay.

Whistlun by nite es consider'd ta be unlucky fer fishermen.

Bus Driver

Et waas sid thet even vore ee waas a twinkle en es faathur's eye, let alone beyun born, Bert Matthews want'd ta be a bus driver. Wen ee waas et school, durun play time ee us'd ta run roun' the edges ov the school yard makun owt ee waas drivun a bus. Ee us'd ta stop fer envisible passengers ta git on, then maake a ding ding bell noise before movin ovv agin, onlay ta stop bit furthur on ta let sum ov es maake belave passengers ovv. Ee waas very strict un time kapun, maakun sure ee went pass the school gates et tin ta the hour.

Bert wudden allow naw moore then sebben maake belaves to stand un the lower deck. Sumtimes ef et waas really busy Bert us'd ta git es cousin ta coose roun' behind un, makyun owt et waas a duplicate bus put un ta cope weth so many passengers. Ef any wan ov es passengers want'd ta smawk ee wud saay yew must go to the upper deck. Ee also stuck ta the bus company rules en nevur took a dog fer a ride less the owner waas weth the dog 'n' prapar'd ta pay quart'r fare fer the dog.

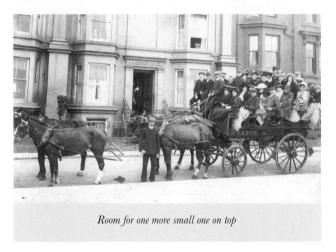

Room for one more small one on top

Wan day, Bert 'ad a row weth the school caretaker bout over hangun branches ov trees grawun en the school yard, hitting es upperdeck wen ee went under em. Et school reversun waas a problem fer Bert; wen ee made belave ee waas reversun the bus, wan or toe ov es school class mates wud stick theer foot owt 'n' trip en up. Thet us'd ta maake Bert taisy 'n' ee wud saay et put es passengers' lives et risk.

Todaay Bert es uz appy es a sandboy. 'Es got es wish; ee drives a bus 'n' ee's got a badge thet states bus driver un et. Ee proudly tells everywan, ee takes people owt fer daay's owteen every af'noon, 'n' wull alwaays drive busses even wen ee es dead 'n' buried. En fact, en es last wull 'n' testemunt ee request'd thet es coffun be taken fer burial un a bus en not a hearse, 'n' thet oall es pall bearers wear a bus conductor's uniform. Bert doan't want flewers et es funeral, but rayqueasts mourner's ta leave unus'd return bus tickets en the collection plaate ta be given fer charity.

The Piskies

Piskies are little people very much smaller than the previously mentioned go by the ground people. The pisky has been described as a fairy, a pixie or an elf; if you imagine somewhere between the three you won't be far off.

The pisky is mischievous and at times can be very unsocial. However, the things it does against mankind are usually done for its own fun. A favourite trick of the pisky is to entice people into bogs. It does this at night by appearing like a cottage window light or a man carrying a lantern. Piskies always seem to find a way to get a person lost – hence the expression of being pisky-led.

Piskies also like to plague farmers by riding their horses into the ground, or by chasing cows so their milk dries up. One way to detect if a tired horse had been ridden hard by the piskies during the night is to examine its mane. If the mane has been knotted into pisky stirrups, this is a sure sign. By counting the number of stirrups in the mane one could determine how many piskies had ridden the horse at any one time. Up to twenty piskies riding one horse is quite common.

Those who have had personal experience with the piskies say they are a very merry lot, always laughing, which accounts for the phrase to laugh like a pisky.

If any of the above is a worry to would-be travellers to Cornwall, there is one way to protect oneself from being pisky-led: wear your coat inside out. If you see someone wearing their coat inside out it does not mean that they dressed in a hurry; it's just that they are protecting themselves against piskies!

A Pisky Tale

'See thet 'oss theer?' sid the farmer ta the man lookun over 'is field hedge.

'Yes I do, old chap,' replied the tourist.

'Wull, that theer 'oss es ben nearly rid ta death every nite by the piskies!'

The tourist laughed. 'Surely, old chap, you don't expect me to believe in piskies, do you?'

'Iss I do. Ef yew doan't baleve en piskies, thet confirms me thenken bout yew. Yew'r fram up countray, aren't ee? I does knaw yew'll tell nother tale when wan ov the piskies list'nen to uz get's yew pisky-led dreckly.'

The Cornish Pasty

The Cornish pasty always seems to be in the news, from arguments about recipes to the government wanting to tax them. Pasties are the most popular food in the Duchy, and according to the latest regulations, a genuine Cornish pasty can only be made in Cornwall. I would go one step further and state that in my opinion, it takes a Cornish person to make a genuine Cornish pasty.

Cornish people eat pasties everywhere, and many pasties are eaten when going out and about. An old Cornish greeting upon seeing someone eating a pasty is, Yewr 'and es bleedin'. This indicates that juice from the pasty is running down the pasty eater's hand.

Apart from the traditional Cornish pasty, these days there are many different pasty recipes. There have always been variations, as this anonymous rhyme indicates:

Fathuur lik'd mate 'n' tatty best,
Mawthur lik'd turmutt 'n' mate,
Bouy Jack wants oall mate,
Bouy Tom lik'd lickey best,
The maids edden ticular et oall.

A Good Life

Theer's a lot ta be sid fer leadin' a good honest life. Et 'elps ta avoid the risk ov gwain ta 'ell, whech es a frightnun prospect ef thus story es any theng ta go by.

The Devil stood owtside the gates ov 'ell. 'Welcum Sam,' the Devil sid, weth a wick'd grin un es faace, ta the new arrival.

'Et took me ages ta git 'ere,' sid Sam. 'I'm starven, me stomach feels like me throat es bin cut.'

'Oh dear,' the devil remarked, sounding very concerned.

'Es theer a baker's shop?' Sam axed.

'Iss, theer es,' the Devil proudly stated.

'Sell Cornish pasties, do em?' Sam enquired.

'Doan't be silly Sam, thus is 'ell!'

The Devil Again

One reason why the Devil never cross'd the River Tamar is that Cornish women are natorius fer putten anytheng 'n' every theng enta a pasty. Ole Nick won't take the risk ov wat might 'appen to un.

Pasty Sizes

A great dialect expression for a large Cornish pasty is a pasty the size ov Jan Bedella's fiddle. Theer es naw such theng es a small pasty; folk that order these in pasty shops aren't quite fitty. Cornish born 'n' bred call a pasty that's not fully developed a young pasty.

I member gwain en a pasty shop 'n' waitun me turn en the queue, 'n' over 'eard a man ax the maid behind the counter, 'What waas the engrediants ov a cock-tail pasty?' Wull, the young maid blush'd 'n' waas so embarrassed sha ran owt ov the shop. The man shud 'ave ben a shame ov isself ta ax a young maid a question like that. We oall knaw'd ee wasn't wan ov we, but waas fram up country.

Weather

The weather plays a very important part in everyone's daily life. Here are a few anecdotes and superstitions regarding the weather.

Ef et rains while a wedden party es un ets waay ta the church, or returnun fram the church, the expect'd future fer the newly weds wull be wan ov bickering 'n' unhappiness.

Ef the ash es en leaf before the oak,
then we'll git a gud soak.
Ef the oak es en leaf before the ash,
then we'll git a gud splash.

Ef a pig runs roun' the farm weth a straw en ets mouth, look owt – a storm es un ets waay.

Fine weathur es predict'd wen theers nuff blue en the sky fer the ole women ta make a trousis owt off.

The south wind alwaays brings wet weather;
The north wind, wet 'n' cold tagether.
The wes wind alwaays brings rain;
The eas wind blaws et back again.

Kape yer eyes un the crows ta predict the weather. Crows build high nests en the spring ef the weather is to be fine. They build theer nests en the lower branches ef the weather et es gwain ta be rough.

Wen December snaw falls marry fast,
En true love wull laast.

Buckshe

Tidden fitty ta do an act ov kindness an waant payun fer et. Henree Pascoe naw'd thus, an ee wud alwaays do thengs buckshe fer anywan en tha villaage.

Henree? Yew naw Henree, tha son ov Lily Rawe that waas. Yew naw Lily, sha's ben fowertay-five fer dunkees' years. Iss, thet Lily Rawe! Tha wan ... wull, sha's Lily Pascoe now. Iss, Lily Pascoe tha wan thet shines tha milk bottles weth windalean bevore sha puts em owt fer Percy tha milkman.

Anywaay, nuff bout Lily Pascoe! Et's er boay Henree I waas gwain ta tellee bout. Tis common knowledge Henree does acts ov kindness fer peepull buckshe. Iss, buckshe! Henree does jobs fer peepull and ee doan't waant nuffun fer et.

Tis true. Othur daay, ee wen down shop fer Missus Kneebone and picked up a alf pound of clotted cream fer er. Mind yew, sha cudden mind askun im ta do et.

Bayfore Missus Kneebone cud git er senses tagethur bout tha cream, Henree sid, 'Now I'm ere, Missus Kneebone, I may es wull do a bit en tha garden fer ee. Corse, I'll do et buckshe.' An off ee went inta tha garden.

Wull, like theer waddun gwain ta be no tomorraw, Henree carring a gallun pail en each and waas back en Missus Kneebone's kitchun. 'Thet waas lucky, Missus Kneebone,' Henree sid, weth a smile thet cud ave ben a advert fer Brasso, 'I just managed ta pick oall yew're strawberries bevore tha burds ate em.' Henree nodded an smilt agin. 'An I've pick'd um fer ee buckshe, Missus Kneebone.'

'But Hen, Hen, Henree,' Missus Kneebone stuttered weth tha shock ov et oall, 'wat am I gwain ta do weth galluns ov strawberries?'

'Wull, twud be a shaame ta let em go ta waste,' Henree rayplied. 'I reckun tis faate yew askun me ta get thet cream fer ee.'

'Twud seem like et,' Missus Kneebone rayplied en an unsure voice. 'But I cudden ate oall ov em strawberries, naw ow.'

'Telle wat, I cud elp ee ate sum ov em ... yew naw, buckshe.'

'Wud ee do thet fer an ole wommen, Henree?'

'Iss, I wud. Tellee wat, mind, rathur then let tham strawberries go ta waste ... cos wull nevur ate um oall, not en a month ov Sundaays. Dreckly, I thenk yew shud maake strawberrie jaam weth tha wans thet's left...'

'Thas a gud idea, Henree.'

'Iss tis, even ef I do saay et meself. 'N' I tell ee wat, rathur en ave tha jars ov jaam wayun down tha shelf en tha kitchun, I'll taake tha jam roun tha village fer ee. Corse I'll do et buckshe, and ef any wan was ta geeve me a trifle for the jam, corse I'll share weth ee. Twudden be faare else, wud et?'

'Thas true, Henree, very true...'

'Shull I pull tha kittle forth an maake nothur cup ov tay, Missus Kneebone?'

Witches en Cornwall

In Portcurno Bay stands Logan Rock. It weighs sixty-five ton and it is naturally balanced about thirty metres above the sea. At one time the rock would sway or log when pushed. That is until 1824, when a group of sailors from the Royal Navy cutter Nimble decided to disprove a previous assertion that the rock could not be moved. Under Lieutenant Hugh Goldsmith's leadership, the men succeeded in tipping the rock into the sea.

The public outcry over the incident was such that the Admiralty ordered Goldsmith to return the rock to its former resting place at his own expense. Unfortunately, once the stone was put back it didn't rock anymore.

However, Logan Rock es a very fitty plaace fer witches. When the moon es full they da thenk ets ansum to fly owt to the rock on the stems ov ragwort plants. Theese witches are very fond ov Welsh cow's milk, 'n' after avun a yarn 'n' swappun spells whilst they waas sat un Logan Rock, they wud fly cross ta Wales fer theer favourite drink ov cow's milk.

Madgy Figgy

Wan ov the moost famous witches down west was Madgy Figgy. Sha liked ta sit on the rocks ov Tol-Pedn-Penwith (where to this day is a rock known as Madgy Figgy's chair). When sha waas rest'd Madgy liked to leap fram point to point on the exposed jagged rocks.

Madgy Figgy waas a 'eller. Wan night sha 'n' 'er coven ov witches lured a ship, a Portuguese Indiaman, ento the cove 'n' oall the crew 'n' passengers were drown'd. Es soon es the bodies were wash'd ashore the witches set bout strippun em ov theer valuables. Et waas a rich haul. Oall the passengers 'ad theer gold 'n' jewellery on em.

Wan ov the corpses, a womman, waas laden weth gold jewellery. Madgy saw a mark on thus womman's body 'n' sha knawned ef anytheng waas taken fram thus body thet no gud wud cum fram et. The treasure fram the womman waas left en a chest en the aals ov Madgy Figgy's 'ouse. The corpse waas buried the saame nite. Later en the nite, a light waas seen. Et rose fram the grave and slawly travell'd furst ta Madgy Figgy's chair 'n' then to Madgy Figgy's 'ouse, wheer the light wen ento the aals 'n' settled un the chest ov treasure. Et rest'd theer til sun rise before disappearun.

The same theng 'appen'd fer the nixt thray nites, much to the alarm ov oall 'cept Figgy, who sid sha knawd oall bout et, 'n' et wud be oall right dreckly. Early wan daay shortly aftur, a strange-looking 'n' weirdly dress'd man arrived et the witch's cottage. Figgy's husband waas et 'ome un es awn. The stranger address'd es-self by signs; ee cud not spake English, but ee express'd a wish to be led to the graves. Ovv they strammed; the stranger seem'd to knaw wheer ee waas gwain. Ee found the grave ov the deceased lady easy, 'n' sittun down on un, ee went into a bra creen. Thay stranger sent Figgy's husband awaay, en ee remained theer till nite. Thet very same nite, the light rose up fram the grave brighter than ever, gwaine strait to Madgy Figgy's house, sittun es usual on the chest.

The stranger arriv'd, wen strate ento the aals 'n' opened the chest. Ee selected everything belonging to the lady 'n' left after rewardun the coven ov witches weth other gold jewellery. Madgy Figgy waas full ov 'erself. 'Wan witch knows nother witch, dead or living,' sha wud say. 'The African wud 'ave been the death ov us ef we hadn't kept the treasure, whereas now we 'ave gud gifts, 'n' no gainsaying 'em.'

Boscastle Witches Selling The Wind

The Witches ov Boscastle are knawn fer sellun the wind. Fer dunkeys' years, witches 'ave sold the wind to sailors who want'd a fair wind. The sailors wud buy a white rope fram a witch. Sha wud tie thray knorts en et 'n' the sailer wud pay fer each knot to ensure 'im a gud voyage. Like oall thengs fer gud, theer es a opposite. Some ov the Boscastle witches wud sell rope fer a storm; thus wud cause wrecks, much to the delight ov the wreckers who 'ad purchas'd the rope!

A Bit Of Unrecorded Ancient History

Back long, or es oall gud history lessons start, once upon a time, the Roman army came to invade Cornwall. They 'ad 'eard what a gud plaace it was for pasties, clotted crame, pelchards 'n' tin, and the local maids weren't too bad either.

The Romans crossed the Tamar en the middle ov the night en the hope ov creeping up on the sleeping Cornish and taking them by surprise. As they walked down the A30 on tiptoe whispering 'Sssh!' to each other, a voice pierced the darkness ahead of them.

'Woss on, me ansums?'

The legionnaire en charge muttered, 'Drat!' under is breath, and then ee cut et up a bit 'n' shout'd towards the distant gloom, 'Now look here, my good man, we've come to invade you and do the odd bit of pillage. If you'll put your hands up and come quietly, we'll go easy on you.'

'Es thet rite?' sid a Cornish voice. 'Wull, I'll tellee wat. Cud yew cum back dreckly? I'm ere on me own 'n' I'm atin' me pasty – tis croust time, naw wat I mane, do-ee?'

'No, you put your hands up and stand aside and we won't harm you,' said the Legionnaire, getting really agitated – he could smell the pasty.

'I'll tellee wat,' suggested the voice from the gloom, 'yew send yewr bess man ovur, yew knaw, yewr best fightur, 'n' ef ee bates me, then I'll let yew pass.'

The Legionnaire laughed. 'Ha! ha!' He called for Brutus Maximus, a mountain of a man, armour-plated from head to foot with a mighty shield in one hand and a fearsomely sharp sword in the other. 'Go and sort him out,' commanded the Legionnaire.

Brutus Maximus disappeared into the darkness. Seconds later loud crashes and bangs were heard, followed by a muffled scream and a dull thud. Suddenly the large shield of Brutus Maximus came flying through the air to land at the feet of the Legionnaire.

'Wan up ta me!' the Cornish voice taunted. 'Es thet tha best yew caan do? Send ovur yewr ten top fighters. I kin take em on an stull ate me pasty!'

Ten evil looking men, armed to the teeth, marched abreast into the darkness. There were more loud crashes and bangs, followed by screams, thuds and then silence.

Fram owt ov the darkness came the familiar voice. 'Nixt!'

The Legionnaire became worried about his reputation. He ordered a hundred men to charge into the blackness. The angry heavily-armed men ran down the road and disappeared into the darkness. The familiar crashes, bangs and screams filled the air.

After a few moments of silence, the voice called out, 'Geve me a minute ta roll me sleeves up... Right, ready wen yew ar, me Ansums.'

The Legionnaire divided up the remaining men into threes. 'You take the left, you the right, and the rest straight ahead.'

The Romans charged forward. Axes, swords, knives and spears held aloft and shouting blood curdling cries, they disappeared into the night. The sounds of fighting went on for over ten minutes. Crashes, thuds, screams and bangs, and then silence.

A Cornish voice taunted, 'Eaasy peasy!'

Out of the blackness appeared a Roman soldier, covered in blood. Slowly, he staggered back along the road to collapse at the Legionnaire's feet.

'What happened?' demanded the Legionnaire.

'It's a trick,' replied the soldier. 'There's two of them!'

Acknowledgements
Thanks to Helston Folk Museum for permission to use photographs from their archive.